Tales of BIRBAL and AKBAR

Retold by
Vernon Thomas

Art work by
Inder Gajjar

Hemkunt Press

A-78 Naraina Indl. Area, Phase-I New Delhi-110028

© Hemkunt Press 1982
Eighth impression 1993

ISBN 81-7010-172-7

Price Rs. 65

Books in this series

Stories from Panchatantra
More stories from Panchatantra
The story of Ramayan
The story of Mahabharata
The story of Krishna
Stories from the Arabian Nights
More Stories from the Arabian Nights
Tales from Indian Mythology
The story of Guru Nanak
Fairy Tales from India
Folk Tales from India
The Story of the Buddha
Story of Mohammad The Prophet
Tales from Indian Classics
Aesop's Fables
Story of Guru Gobind Singh
Being a Sikh
Sindbad the Sailor
Legends From Northern India
Story of Jesus Christ
Gogo the Dancing mule
Stories of Gopal Bhand
Tales from India
Bedtime Stories from India
Tales of Birbal & Akbar
Story of Maharaja Ranjit Singh
More Tales from Indian Classics
Biography of Guru Nanak
The Story of Baha 'u' llah
The Prophets of God
Story of Hanuman
South Indian Folk Tales
Tales from Eastern India
Folk Tales from Mauritius
Jatak Tales
Two stories from the Arabian Nights

Printed by Jay Print Pack Private Limited, New Delhi-110015

INTRODUCTION

Among the Moghul kings who ruled India at one time, Akbar was perhaps the greatest. A remarkable ruler, under his guidance India prospered greatly. Akbar had all the best qualities to be loved and respected by his subjects. He was good and kind, wise and just, understanding and tolerant, and a lot else. During his reign Hindus and Muslims lived in peace. Akbar encouraged talent, and the arts did well. He was quick to recognise ability, and give ability a chance to prove itself.

It is no wonder, therefore that Akbar respected Birbal for his great wisdom and abilities. Birbal was a Hindu, but this made no difference to the king. In fact, it is a true example of Akbar's great tolerance. From the moment they met almost, Akbar realised Birbal was a very special person. Birbal became a close friend and a great favourite. He was a precious pearl at Akbar's Court. He helped his king so much, that Akbar depended on him in all matters.

Birbal was well known for his great wit. He was kind and just to the poor. They came to him with their problems and he helped them. As a result, he grew famous, while as often happens, his fame and the favour he was shown by the king earned him enemies amongst Akbar's ministers and courtiers.

He dealt with his own problems, with his own same wit and wisdom that he used to solve the problems of his king and the people. But, no doubt, the stories in this book will explain all this more clearly.

Tales of Birbal and Akbar are amongst the most popular and best-loved stories and legends of India. They have delighted both children and grownups for years now, and will continue to do so for many more to come.

Vernon Thomas

Contents

1. How Akbar met Birbal — 7
2. Birbal arrives at Akbar's Palace — 13
3. Greater than Lord Indra — 23
4. Birbal solves the Case — 27
5. The Butcher and the Grain Merchant — 33
6. The Two Flour Merchants — 39
7. The Widow's Savings — 51
8. The Old Woman and the Judge — 62
9. The Dishonest Tailor — 67
10. The Most Foolish Men in Delhi — 74
11. Unlucky Chand — 82
12. The Prince and the Traveller — 88
13. Birbal makes Enemies — 96
14. Akbar sets a Task — 100

How Akbar met Birbal

When Akbar was still quite a young king, one day he went hunting in a certain forest with some of his friends. He was very fond of hunting, and would hunt often. On this occasion, he had heard that there was plenty of good game to be found in this forest. As such, both he and his friends were looking forward to shooting many animals.

It was a hot summer's day, but no one minded the heat. All were most eager to begin their sport. Yet, as they rode along, they grew slowly disappointed. There was not a single animal to be seen.

"Really!" remarked Akbar. "Whoever said this forest was good for hunting, must have been joking."

Still, in spite of not finding anything, quite hopeful, they continued to search, while the sun grew hotter and hotter. Soon everyone was thirsty.

Now, they began to search for a stream or a pond, so that they could drink some water. But even here they were not successful.

"We must find a village," suggested one of the men. "We are sure to find water there."

As this was a good idea, Akbar and his friends rode faster. As they went along, all of a sudden they spotted a small boy. He was carrying a bundle of twigs.

"Listen, young fellow!" called out Akbar, as they drew close. "Is there a village close by? We want some water to drink."

"Yes, Sir, the village where I live is not far from here," answered the boy. "We have a tank, with plenty of water."

"Then please take us to it," said Akbar.

"Certainly!" agreed the boy, and one of the men now lifted him up on to his horse, and together they all rode along.

Soon they reached the village where the boy lived. The boy took them to the tank. He was very helpful. He went off and filled a jug, and gave them all to drink, one by one, as they got off their horses and sat down to rest.

When it came to Akbar's turn, Akbar took a good look at the boy. He was a bright little fellow, Akbar thought.

"What is your name?" he asked him.

"What is your name? You tell me first, then I'll tell you," answered the boy boldly.

Akbar was surprised. No one had ever dared to speak to him that way.

"Do you know who I am?" he demanded angrily.

"Do you know who I am?" the boy replied with a smile.

Instead of growing more angry, Akbar began to laugh. He had a great sense of humour, and he quite

liked the cheeky young fellow. Slipping off a diamond ring from one of his fingers, he handed it to the boy, saying:

"Here! Take a look at this. It will tell you who I am."

Small as he was, the boy at once recognised the royal seal on the ring. He realised, this was the king he was talking to. He was so surprised that he could not speak.

Akbar was quite amused to see him look so upset. "When you grow up, little fellow," he said, "come and visit me at my palace in Delhi. Bring this ring with you, so that I will know you." And with that he climbed up on his horse again, and rode away with his friends.

The boy was by now busy examining the beautiful ring. He hardly noticed that the king and his friends had gone. Till they were almost out of sight. But quite delighted, he returned home now and showed the ring to his mother.

His mother was very pleased to see the ring, more pleased when she heard who had given it to him, though she was quite upset, when her son told her what he had said to the king.

"You should not have been so bold," she scolded him. "You should have told the king your name was Mahesh Das."

Then next moment she smiled, as she thought of the wonderful future that awaited her son, when he was old enough to accept the king's invitation. She hoped he would be very famous some day.

"Mahesh," she said, "you are a clever boy. You must study hard. When you grow up, you must do as the king says. He is sure to help you to become famous."

"Yes, Ma, I will go to the king's palace in Delhi, when I grow up," agreed Mahesh. "I will show the king this ring, and he will know me".

"Very good!" smiled his mother. "But you had better give that ring to me to keep, till you are old enough to look after it. If you were to lose it, the king might not remember you."

Obediently, Mahesh handed over the ring. Like most children, as he grew up, at times he forgot about it. But he studied hard, and grew learned and wise. He well earned the name which he came to be known by later. This was Birbal, which means wise.

Birbal arrives at Akbar's Palace

By the time Mahesh had completed his studies, he was quite a young man. His mother decided it was time for him to accept King Akbar's invitation.

"My son, you are grown up now," she said. "You are good and clever. I am proud of you. It is my greatest wish to see you become famous some day. It is time for you to visit King Akbar. Don't forget to take the ring he gave you, so that he will know you."

Mahesh readily agreed to go. Though he was sad to leave home, he set out soon for Delhi. It was a long and tiring journey. He was quite weary, by the time he reached Delhi. As he walked through the streets of the capital city, he forgot his tiredness. He was so charmed by all he saw. Being a village boy, he had never visited a city before. As such, the streets and houses were all so new to him. He could only stare in wonder.

At last, he reached the gates of King Akbar's palace. He asked the guard on duty to let him enter, but the man refused.

"Why?" asked Mahesh. "I know that the king meets his people quite freely. You cannot stop me from going in."

"I can stop you!" answered the guard rudely. "I decide who enters and who does not." And then he added in a whisper: "But if you give me something I will let you in."

"You mean you want me to give you some money?" asked Mahesh, surprised at the man's dishonesty. "I don't have any money." Next moment he went on, as an idea came into his mind: "But if you let me meet the king, who knows, His Majesty may be pleased with me! He might reward me. In which case, I can pay you later."

"Very good!" agreed the guard. "I will let you in. But don't forget. You must give me half of whatever the king gives you as a gift."

"I will give you half of whatever the king gives me as a gift," promised Mahesh, and with that the guard opened the gates.

As he walked through the palace gardens, Mahesh was struck with wonder. He had never seen the like before. Everywhere marble fountains sprayed water gracefully. Flowers of all colours bloomed in well-kept flower beds. While the grass beneath his feet was so green and well-trimmed, it looked like a carpet.

The palace which lay beyond was more wonderful. It had tall stately minarets and a great dome, while once inside, Mahesh thought he must be dreaming. Never had he imagined that King Akbar's home could be so grand! For there were huge marble halls, with high roofs and carved pillars. The floors were of marble, too. They were shining and spotless.

The throne room which be entered next quite took his breath away. All around were signs of great wealth. There were heavy curtains, in a deep shade of red. On the floor was a great carpet, in a many-coloured design. At the far end of the room, on a throne of gold, studded with precious stones, sat King Akbar, resting against cushions of pink satin.

The king was dressed in a tunic and trousers of sky blue, a silver turban on his head. He wore a necklace of diamonds, while several precious stones sparkled from the rings he had on his fingers. He looked so great, seated there, surrounded by his colour-fully-dressed courtiers, that Mahesh could hardly recognise him as the person he had once met.

Mahesh grew just a little nervous, though since he was a brave young man, he soon recovered. He joined the crowd of courtiers, waiting for a chance to speak to the king. Then when he found one, as he drew close to the throne, he took out the ring which Akbar had given him.

"Sire !" he said, showing Akbar the ring. "No doubt, you will recognise this !"

"Of course I recognise that ring, and I know you, too," answered Akbar at once. "You are that little boy I met years ago. I am glad you have remembered my invitation. I am pleased to see you."

Akbar invited Mahesh to sit down. He began to question him about his studies, and what he had been doing since last they had met. From the answers he received, Akbar was quick to mark that Mahesh was learned and wise.

"Well, my young friend," he said at last, feeling very pleased, "you must tell me what I can do for you ! Ask me any favour and I will grant it."

"Sire, that is very kind of you," answered Mahesh. "I desire that you order me to be given a hundred whip lashes."

"A hundred whip lashes ! Is that what you asked for ?" cried Akbar, quite puzzled, while all present were most amazed to hear this strange request.

"I did indeed, Sire!" smiled Mahesh. "A hundred whip lashes is what I desire."

"But I cannot grant such a request!" said Akbar. "That would be punishment, not a favour. You have done nothing wrong."

But Mahesh insisted. "I assure you, Sire, to me a hundred whip lashes will be a great favour, not a punishment."

Seeing him so determined, Akbar agreed. He sent for one of his soldiers. He ordered that Mahesh be given a hundred whip lashes before all present. And while this was being done, Akbar could not help but think, that the young man must be quite out of his mind. He wondered how he could have thought him to be learned and wise.

However, as the soldier delivered the fiftieth lash, across Mahesh's bare back, Mahesh raised his hands and called to him to stop.

"No doubt, you have realised you are being foolish!" remarked Akbar.

But Mahesh shook his head. "No, Sire! The balance fifty lashes must be given, but not to me," he explained. "You see, when I arrived at your palace gates a short while ago, the guard on duty let me enter, on the condition I share with him half of whatever I receive from you as a gift. As such, the balance fifty lashes are rightfully his."

Akbar was surprised to hear of the dishonesty of one of his staff. At the same time he quite understood now the reason for Mahesh's strange request. He began to laugh, and ordered that the guard be brought at once.

The guard wondered why he was wanted by the king and grew afraid, when he found that Mahesh had reported his dishonesty. And when he was told what was to be his share of the bargain, he could hardly believe his ears. He began to beg for mercy. But Akbar refused. He ordered that the punishment to be given without a moment's delay.

When it was over, Akbar said to the guard: "I hope that will teach you a lesson." And turning to Mahesh next, he went on, with a smile:

"Since you are truly wise, Mahesh, I have decided to change your name. From today you will be known as Birbal. From today you will stay at the palace, so that we may get to know each other better."

Greater than Lord Indra

Living at the palace, Birbal was able to meet the king often. Though Akbar was a busy ruler, he always found time to chat with Birbal. Since both were learned men, they had plenty to talk about. The more they discussed, Akbar realised more and more that Birbal would be of great use to him.

Akbar grew very fond of Birbal. He soon gave him money and land. Thus Birbal was able to live comfortably, like the other courtiers and ministers.

One day Akbar invited some of his close friends to dinner. As can be expected, the meal was a real feast, with many tasty dishes being served. Several courtiers and ministers were present. Birbal was included, as well. He sat close to the king.

When they had finished eating, a story-teller was brought in to entertain the guests. The story-teller had some wonderful tales to tell. He told them so well, that everyone listened with great interest—Akbar, chiefly, since he loved to hear stories. At the end, when the story-teller had finished, Akbar was so pleased, that he gave him a bag of gold coins as a gift.

The man was so full of gratitude, that at once he bowed before Akbar and declared: "Truly Sire, you are the greatest king that ever lived! In fact, you are greater than Indra, the great Lord of heaven."

"Thank you!" smiled Akbar, very pleased. He was too wise, of course, to believe such a thing. But as the story-teller left the room, to have some fun, he turned to his guests, and asked if they agreed with what the man had said.

No doubt, all those present did not agree. A man could never be greater than a god! they knew. But as they were afraid of offending the king, they just nodded and said not a word, looking quite worried.

"Well, I am pleased you all think I am greater than a god!" remarked Akbar slyly, for he could tell from their faces that they thought quite the opposite. As such he went on: "Tell me, why do you think this?"

The guests, courtiers and ministers grew more upset now. They did not know what to say. Each looked at the other, hoping someone would reply. But no one did.

At last Akbar turned to Birbal. "Tell me, Birbal, do you think I am greater than Lord Indra?"

"But certainly!" answered Birbal at once, to the surprise of everyone, Akbar included. And he went on to explain, without hesitation: "It is because, Sire, you can do something Lord Indra cannot! You can send a wicked man out of your kingdom. But Lord Indra cannot send anyone out of his. Since he owns the Universe, where would he send such a man? As such you are greater."

Everyone laughed heartily at this clever answer. While Akbar enjoyed the joke, his liking for Birbal increased. He was glad Birbal did not flatter. Rather, he could turn flattery into fun.

Birbal solves the Case

As Birbal got used to his new way of life, he soon began to attend the court. He would be present, along with the other courtiers and ministers when Akbar saw to the business of the government. At such times, also, Akbar would receive the people, and help them to solve their problems.

One day two men appeared before Akbar. One was an honest merchant, and the other, a cheat. While the merchant was a rich man, the cheat was also rich. But he had made his money by cheating other rich people.

The cheat had a special way for doing this. He would make friends with rich people, posing as a good and honest man. Then when he had won their confidence, he would cheat them. He would do so very cleverly, with the result, that so far he had not been caught.

On this occasion, he had made friends with the merchant in the same way. When he had won the merchant's confidence, he invited the merchant to his house one night for dinner. Since the merchant thought him to be a good friend, gladly he went along. Some of the cheat's friends were present at the dinner. There was plenty to eat and drink, plenty of fun and laughter. The merchant returned home that night very pleased.

However, the next morning he was amazed, when the cheat arrived at his house, accusing him of having stolen a costly diamond. The merchant told him he was mistaken, but the cheat would not have it. He insisted that the merchant either return the diamond, or pay for it.

Since the merchant refused, the cheat took the matter to Akbar. As witnesses, he took along four of his friends who had been present at the dinner. All four said that the merchant had stolen the diamond.

Akbar listened to the stories of both parties. At the end, he did not know whom to believe. In spite of the four witnesses, he felt the merchant was not guilty. He looked an honest sort.

Noticing Birbal standing close by, Akbar turned to him and said : "Birbal, you have heard everything. Can you say who is guilty in this case ?"

"I will try, Sire ! Let me think," answered Birbal quietly.

After a bit, Birbal asked for some clay to be brought. When this was done, he divided the clay into four parts, handing one to each witness. Then he said to them :

"Now, you have all seen this diamond which the merchant has stolen. So, I am putting you into separate rooms. I want each of you to shape your lump of clay into diamond, like the one you saw."

Four court attendants now came forward and led the four witnesses away. The result was, that soon each witness found himself alone in a room, with a lump of clay, which he did not know what to do with. In truth, not one of the four had ever seen a diamond. They had been bribed by the cheat to appear as witnesses.

It happened, each of the four belonged to a different trade. While one was a barber, another was a tailor. The third was a carpenter; the fourth was a butcher.

As the barber wondered what to do, suddenly he remembered his father having told him that, as a barber, his razor was as precious to him as a diamond. A diamond must look like a razor, he decided, therefore, and shaped his piece of clay accordingly.

The tailor, whilst thinking deeply, remembered his mother having said that, as a tailor, his needle was as valuable to him as a diamond. As such, reasoning like the barber, he made a needle out of clay.

In the same way, the carpenter remembered his grandmother once advising him to guard his saw, as he would a diamond. So he made his clay into a saw, while the butcher turned his into a knife, as he remembered his grandfather having told him, a butcher's knife was as dear to a butcher as a diamond.

When they were quite finished, the four were brought before Akbar again, to show what the stolen diamond had looked like.

"It is clear those men have never seen a diamond, Sire!" pointed out Birbal, glancing at the four clay models.

"Yes, and it is clear who is lying," spoke Akbar sternly. And at once he ordered the cheat to be put into prison.

All present praised Birbal highly, for the clever way had solved the case. As the news spread, Birbal began to be well-known, while Akbar began to seek his help in such matters often.

The Butcher and the Grain Merchant

A butcher one day sat in his shop, selling meat to his customers. Since there were many present at the time, he was kept very busy. He cut and he chopped away, dealing with each one's order, in turn. The money he received from the sales, he put into a canvas bag, which he kept beside him.

As he finished with the last customer, the butcher thought he would rest a while. But along came a grain merchant now ! He ordered some meat, which the butcher cut, and was about to hand over. When, to his great surprise, the man grabbed his money bag all of a sudden, and prepared to pay for the meat from it.

"What are you doing ?" demanded the butcher. "You have taken my money bag."

"Your money bag !" cried the grain merchant. "This is my money bag. I have just taken it out to pay you."

"Thief !" shouted the butcher angrily, and jumping up he seized the grain merchant by the neck.

The grain merchant clung to the bag and shouted for help. Hearing his cries, some people soon gathered.

"What is happening?" they wanted to know.

"This man is trying to steal my money bag!" accused the grain merchant.

"Your money bag! It is my money bag!" shouted the butcher in great anger. "You are a thief."

As they continued to accuse each other, saying the bag was his, those looking on could not decide to whom the bag really belonged.

"Let us take them to the king," suggested one man. "Let the king decide who is the true owner."

"Why, the king? He is always so busy," pointed out another. "Let us take them to his man called Birbal. You must have heard of Birbal. He helps the king in such matters, I hear. He is very clever, I believe."

As the others all agreed to this, the two soon found themselves before Birbal. Birbal listened patiently to what both had to say. He asked to see the money bag.

"I swear to you by the Holy Quoran that this bag is mine," declared the grain merchant, as he handed it over.

Birbal took the bag, and without a word left the room. On his own, in a quiet spot, he emptied out the bag, examining both its inner and outer sides carefully. He examined the money, which had been in the bag, next. At last, he put the money back, held the bag to his nose for a second, and then returned with it to where the others awaited him.

"When you took it out to pay the butcher, was he able to grab it out of your hand?" Birbal wanted to know.

"He tried to, but I held on to it tight, so he was not able to touch it," answered the grain merchant proudly.

"In that case," said Birbal, "can you tell me how this bag comes to smell of raw meat? Also, can you explain the small animal bloodstains, which I noticed on the inner side of the bag, and on some of the coins?"

Hearing this the grain merchant grew afraid. He knew he had been caught out. As he failed to answer, Birbal turned to the butcher.

"I know this bag is yours," he said to him. "The smell and the blood stains tell me, you touch the raw meat, and then accept money, without washing your hands in between."

As the butcher confirmed that he was in the habit of doing that, Birbal returned him his money bag. He ordered that the grain merchant be taken to prison.

The grain merchant begged for mercy. He promised he would never do such a thing again. But Birbal shook his head.

"How can I forgive you, when you swore by the Holy Quoran that the bag was yours? That is more serious even than stealing," he pointed out.

"He deserves to be punished," agreed those who had brought the two men to him, while, when these went away, they told everyone they met what a clever person Birbal was.

In this way Birbal grew famous.

The Two Flour Merchants

In the city of Delhi there lived two flour merchants named Mashood and Mehmood. They had known each other for many years, and were good friends. However, while Mashood was honest, Mehmood was dishonest. Alas, Mashood knew nothing about this bad quality in his friend!

The two did good business. But one day Mehmood faced great trouble. He found himself very short of money. His position was so bad, that his business was in danger of failing. Most upset, he went to Mashood for help.

"My friend," he explained, "though I feel ashamed to ask, do please lend me five hundred gold pieces. I am in great trouble. If I don't get this money, I will have to close down my business. But if you help me, I promise to return it as soon as I am able to."

"But, surely I will lend you the money," agreed Mashood at once. "I am glad you asked. I will let you have it right away." And opening his money box, he took out the sum and handed it over.

"Thank you ! Thank you !" said Mehmood gratefully. "I shall give you a receipt for this sum."

But Mashood began to laugh. "A receipt !" he cried. "That will not be necessary. You are my friend, and I trust you. You may return the money when you are able to. I'm in no hurry."

After thanking him again, Mehmood left. In a short while he had made up his losses. His business did well once more. However, he did not trouble to return the loan he had taken. In fact, he decided not to. His dishonesty getting the better of him, he reasoned that, since no receipt had been given, there was no proof. Besides, as time passed, and Mashood did not remind him about the money, he thought Mashood must have forgotten.

Mashood had not forgotten, however. He certainly remembered. But patient and trusting as he was, he felt that Mehmood would return the money, sooner or later. Besides, he felt shy to ask for it.

Thus, a very long time passed, and the money was still due. Since Mehmood did not even mention it, Mashood decided there was no other way but to ask.

"Mehmood." he said, therefore, when next they met. "much as I hate to remind you, when do you expect to return me those five hundred gold pieces, you borrowed so long ago ?"

But Mehmood now pretended he knew nothing about the loan. "Five hundred gold pieces!" he cried. "When did I borrow five hundred gold pieces from you? You are making a mistake, my friend! It must have been someone else."

"No! No! I am not mistaken!" answered Mashood, in some surprise. "I certainly lent you five hundred gold pieces." And though he tried hard to get his friend to remember, Mehmood continued to deny having borrowed the money. Sadly, at last, Mashood decided that indeed Mehmood was dishonest, while the more he thought about this, the sadder he grew.

"What is the matter?" asked his wife that evening, noticing he was so upset. "Tell me what is troubling you?"

But Mashood said it was nothing. After all, he did not want his wife to think badly of his friend. Still, his wife refused to believe that nothing was wrong. She kept on insisting, and at last Mashood told her.

"You did not tell me that this man borrowed money from you?" she scolded him at the end.

"Since it was a business matter, I kept it a secret," explained Mashood "But what should I do? There is no receipt. How can I prove it? Still, I cannot afford to lose such a large sum."

"You must do something," spoke his wife firmly. "Go to a judge. Make a case against this man." And then she went on, as a bright idea came to her mind. "Better still! Go to Birbal. You know how wise he is. He helps so many people. He will surely find a way to help you."

As such, Mashood went to Birbal and told him his story. He asked Birbal what he should do.

"Do! wonder what you can do!" answered Birbal thoughtfully. "You have no receipt. There is no proof. But give me a little time to think. I shall try to solve your problem."

Mashood thanked Birbal and returned home, feeling a bit easier in mind. He was hopeful, that Birbal would help him to get his money back.

Meanwhile Birbal sent for Mehmood, and questioned him about the money he owed Mashood. Mehmood, of course, denied having taken any money.

"This is a great lie!" he cried. "This man calls himself my friend, and he accuses me falsely! If I have taken any money from him, ask him to show you the receipt. If he can, I will certainly pay him."

"There is no receipt," answered Birbal quietly. "This Mashood says he trusted you. If you have taken the money, return it."

But Mehmood protested more strongly, that he had not taken any money from Mashood. So seeing there was nothing he could do at that moment, to prove who was guilty, Birbal told him he could go.

However, Birbal now thought over the problem deeply. He made up his mind as to what to do. A few days later, therefore, without letting one know about the other, he sent the two a barrel of flour each. He wrote each a letter, asking them as a favour to sell the flour for him, and send him the money from the sale.

Mashood and Mehmood agreed readily to oblige. While Mashood reasoned, he must help someone who was trying to help him, Mehmood at once thought about making a profit on the sale.

The two soon opened their barrels. And imagine their surprise, when each discovered a gold coin in the flour in his barrel! The coins, of course, had been placed there by Birbal on purpose, to test the honesty of the two men.

However, seeing the coin, Mashood thought at once: "Dear me! This coin must have fallen into the flour by mistake. I must return it to Birbal." And off he went at once. He met Birbal and returned the coin, explaining about it.

Birbal pretended to be surprised. "No really!" he cried. "This is most honest of you. I did not know about that coin. It must have fallen into the flour by mistake. Thank you very much for returning it to me!"

Birbal now waited to see if Mehmood would come to return his gold coin. However, Mehmood had other ideas. No sooner did he set eyes on the coin, than he exclaimed aloud:

"Now, if this isn't a piece of luck! A gold coin in this barrel of flour!"

"A gold coin in the flour!" cried his small son, who happened to be present.

"Yes! Yes!" said Mehmood eagerly. "Now take this gold coin to your mother, and tell her to keep it safely." And as he handed it over, the small boy went off to do as he was told.

Both Mashood and Mehmood soon sold their barrels of flour, which fetched a good price. But whilst Mashood sent Birbal the full amount he had got from his sale, Mehmood kept a part for himself from his, and sent only the balance.

Since the flour in both barrels had been of the same quality and quantity, Birbal at once noticed that Mehmood had given him less money. Since Mehmood had not returned the gold coin, as well, Birbal was quite certain that he was dishonest.

As such Birbal now sent for the two. When they arrived, whilst thanking them for having sold the flour for him, he at once pointed out to Mehmood, that he had given him less money from his sale.

"But that is not correct!" denied Mehmood. "I sold the flour, and gave you the full amount I received."

"Well," Birbal informed him. "I sent your friend here a similar barrel of flour, and he gave me more money. As such, I know you paid me less. Also, I had a gold coin put into each of the barrels. Your friend returned me the one he found in his, but you have not returned the one which was in yours."

Hearing this Mehmood pretended to be most amazed. "A gold coin in the flour!" he exclaimed.

"But I found no gold coin, I promise. I opened the barrel in front of my small son. Even he can say there was no gold coin."

"Well, in that case, I might have been mistaken," said Birbal. "I'll just go and find out. Perhaps, my servant forgot to put the gold coin into your barrel!" And with that he left the room.

Birbal, however, went and called one of his servants. He told him to go in secret to Mehmood's house, and fetch Mehmood's small son.

"Tell the boy," instructed Birbal, "that his father wants him to bring that gold coin, which was found in the barrel of flour."

The servant rushed off. He soon returned with the boy, who quite innocently brought the gold coin with him. As the boy was brought into the room, Mehmood was surprised to see him. He was more surprised when his son said :

"Here, Abba! Here is the gold coin which you wanted."

"What are you doing here? What are you talking about?" demanded Mehmood, in both alarm and anger.

"You sent for me, Abba!" explained the boy simply. You ordered me to bring the gold coin, which you found in that barrel of flour."

"There was no gold coin in that barrel of flour!" shouted Mehmood staring angrily at the boy.

But the boy did not understand. He repeated that indeed, there had been. He reminded his father of how he had asked him to take the coin, and give it to his mother to keep.

Since the truth was out now, Mehmood could hardly continue to deny having found the coin.

"Well, that certainly proves it," decided Birbal now. "If you can be dishonest about a single gold coin, you can be dishonest about five hundred such. Make sure you pay this man what you owe him, or I will have you punished."

Hearing this Mehmood now confessed. He begged Birbal's pardon. He promised to pay at once.

Mashood was delighted to get his money back. He was very grateful to Birbal.

The Widow's Savings

In a certain village there lived an old widow. She had lost her husband when she was quite young. She had no children, and was quite alone in the world. She had to work very hard to support herself. She scrubbed pots and pans in several houses; she swept floors and washed down courtyards, and in this way she earned her living.

Since she was a wise woman, the widow realised that one day she would grow too old to work. She would require money to keep herself. As such she was very careful. Over the years, she had saved a good part of her earnings, with the result, that she had collected five hundred gold coins, which she kept in a hole in the floor of her hut.

As she was getting on in years, and felt she might die soon, the widow decided to go on a pilgrimage, to the holy city of Kashi. She wished to pray there and to do penance for her sins. But the problem was her savings. She felt she could not leave them in her hut, as they might be stolen in her absence. At the same time, she did not wish to take them with her, in case she was robbed on the journey.

The widow thought over this problem for a while. At last she decided to leave her savings in the care of a certain Brahmin. This man was known to be very holy and honest. He would look after her money while she was away.

Quite pleased with her decision, the widow went off and met the Brahmin. She made her request. But the Brahmin shook his head.

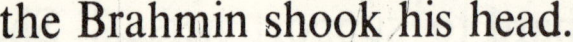

"My good woman, I am a holy man," he pointed out. "I have no use for money. Why do you wish to burden me with this problem? If someone were to steal your money, you would blame me. Where would I get the money to replace it?"

But the widow continued to plead, till, at last, the Brahmin agreed.

"All right!" he answered. "I will do as you wish. But I will not touch your money. Put your gold coins into a cloth bag and stitch it up. Then bring the bag and bury it under the banyan tree, where I sit and pray every day. When you return from your pilgrimage, you can dig up the bag. But, I repeat, I will not touch your money."

In great relief, the old widow agreed to this. She went home, removed her savings and put them into a bag made of strong cloth. Carefully she stitched up the opening of the bag, using a thick needle and stout thread. When she was ready, she took the bag and buried it under the banyan tree, in the Brahmin's presence.

"Well, there you are!" said the Brahmin, when she had quite finished. "Your savings will remain there till you return."

The widow thanked him warmly and left. She was away for a very long time, in fact, much longer than she expected. As such, as the months crept by and she did not return, the Brahmin began to think she must have died. The more he thought about this, he grew tempted to steal her gold.

Finally, one dark night, the Brahmin dug up the bag in secret. Removing the five hundred gold coins, he put five hundred silver ones of little value into the bag. Early next morning he took the bag to the village tailor, and got him to stitch up the opening again firmly. Thereafter, he reburied the bag in the same spot, as if it had never been touched.

The Brahmin was pleased with himself. He felt quite rich. Carefully, he hid the five hundred gold coins. As time passed, he got over a feeling of guilt, for having helped himself to the old woman's money.

However, one morning to his amazement, the widow returned, and came to meet him. The Brahmin stared at her in disbelief. He thought he was seeing a ghost ; but she was real, of course.

"No doubt, you are surprised to see me. You must have thought I was dead," she said with a smile. "But I am sorry for over-staying. I liked Kashi so much, that I found it difficult to leave. If I had taken my savings with me, I would not have returned."

"Well, your savings are where you left them." said the Brahmin, feeling rather uncomfortable.

The widow now went to the spot where she had buried her money. Recovering the bag, she found it outwardly quite intact. Thinking her gold was safe, she thanked the Brahmin warmly and returned to her home. Then a little later, she sat down to open the bag. She removed a part of the stitching over the opening, and poured out the coins. And as she saw them, she was most upset and surprised to find, that they were of silver and not gold.

'This Brahmin has robbed me.' she said to herself, as she began to weep. But soon, her tears turned into anger. Off she went and met the Brahmin. Eyes flashing in rage she demanded :

"I buried a bag of five hundred gold coins. Now I find the bag contains five hundred silver coins. Can you explain how such a thing has happened ?"

But the Brahmin now looked at her coldly, and pointed out : "You found your bag in the same spot, didn't you ? You found the stitching on it quite intact, didn't you ?" And as she nodded that, indeed, she had, he went on, with a shrug : "Then how can you question me in this matter ? Are you trying to say I am a thief ? That I have stolen your gold coins ?"

"But I think you are the thief," he went on after a pause. "You buried silver coins instead of gold, with the idea of accusing me falsely on your return."

He pretended to be very hurt and very angry. He began to shout. Hearing him a crowd soon collected. The Brahmin turned to inform those gathered, that the old widow had accused him wrongly. While the widow insisted that the Brahmin had cheated her. But, alas, no one believed her!

"You are lying!" some of the onlookers said to her. "We know this man to be good and honest." And with that, they chased her away in anger.

The poor widow was quite beside herself with worry. She returned to her hut and sat down and wept again. She saw herself soon dying of hunger and poverty. Oh, who would help her? She wondered. And then, all of a sudden, she remembered!

'Birbal! Birbal will help me!' she said to herself, and drying her tears, she hurried off to meet him.

Birbal received her with all due kindness. He listened to her tale of woe. When she had finished speaking, he asked to see the bag in which she had kept her money. Luckily, the widow had thought of bringing it with her. She handed it over at once.

Birbal examined the bag. He studied the stitching over the opening, and then said:

"From what remains of this stitching, I can tell this is the work of a tailor—a good one, who knows his job. Do you have a tailor in your village?"

"Yes, Sir!" she answered. "There is only one tailor, and he is very good at his work."

"Hm!" grunted Birbal, and he fell to thinking.

Leave this bag with me," he said after a bit, "Come back the day after tomorrow, and I will let you know about your money."

The widow thanked him and left, feeling better already. Meanwhile Birbal ordered one of his servants to go and meet the tailor of the village, where the old woman lived.

"When you find this man, tell him that I wish to see him at once," instructed Birbal.

The servant went off. He found the tailor, and gave him Birbal's message. While the tailor wondered why Birbal should want him, he hurried along to meet Birbal at once. He was trembling, by the time he was brought before Birbal.

Birbal at once noticed that he was afraid. "My good man," he said to him kindly, "if you speak the truth, you have no reason to fear. Tell me, do you remember ever sewing up a bag containing some coins ?"

At first the man frowned. But as Birbal showed him the bag, he soon remembered.

"Yes!" he nodded. "That is my stitching, all right. Some time ago, I remember, the Brahmin who sits under the banyan tree in the village brought this bag to me. He asked me to stitch up the opening. He paid me well for doing so."

"Do you remember, if the bag contained gold coins?" asked Birbal.

"Oh, no!" The tailor shook his head firmly. "I remember the bag contained silver coins. I remember this very well. Because I wondered at the time, why the Brahmin should wish to take such care of a bag, which contained coins that were of little value."

Birbal thanked the tailor and told him he could go. Now he sent for the Brahmin; and when he arrived, Birbal accused him straight away of stealing the widow's gold.

The Brahmin strongly denied having done such a thing. But Birbal showed him the bag, and told him about the tailor. As such, he soon had to admit that he was guilty.

"What have you done with the gold?" damanded Birbal.

"I have kept it, Sir" answered the Brahmin, hanging his head in shame.

"Then you must return it," ordered Birbal. "Bring it to me at once ! Or else, you know what will happen to you !"

In great fear the Brahmin went off, and soon came back with the money. He handed it over to Birbal. As such, when the widow called later, Birbal was able to return her the five hundred gold coins.

The old widow was delighted. She was very grateful to Birbal. She went off, praising him highly. She told everyone she met what he had done for her. And Birbal grew more famous.

The Old Woman and the Judge

One day an old woman came to see Birbal.

"Sir, you must help me!" she begged of him. "I have just returned after visiting my daughter, who lives quite far away. Before I left home, I gave my jewels to a judge who lives in my village, to keep for me while I was away. But yesterday when I went and asked back for my jewels, this judge denies having received them. He accused me of trying to cheat him. My jewels are all I have, Sir! I was keeping them to give to my granddaughter when she grows up. Do try and get them back for me!"

Seeing her so upset, Birbal told the old woman not to worry. "I will try my best to help you," he promised. "Just give me this judge's name and address. Then go home, and come back tomorrow and see me."

Gladly the old woman gave the details asked for. She went away, feeling quite sure that Birbal would solve her problem. Meanwhile Birbal fetched some notepaper and a pen. He sat down and wrote a letter to the judge. He sealed it, and sent one of his servants to deliver it. The servant soon returned to say he had done so.

"Very good!" said Birbal, and told him he could go.

Next day the old woman arrived to see Birbal. She was very excited. She hoped to hear good news. As such she was quite disappointed, when Birbal said to her:

"Go and meet that judge right away. Ask him again to return your jewels."

"Is that all?" she cried. "I have already asked him many times, and he has refused. If I go again, he is sure to get angry and turn me out."

But Birbal repeated quietly: "I want you to go and ask that judge for your jewels."

Seeing he was so determined, the old woman went off to do as he said.

'I cannot understand how people say this Birbal helps everyone,' she grumbled to herself. 'He has done nothing to help me.'

However, some hours later, she returned in a very joyful mood. She was clutching her box of jewels, and could hardly stop praising Birbal.

"Sir, I must thank you! I am so very grateful," she said to Birbal, when they met. I don't know how you did it, but that judge returned my jewels, the moment I asked for them."

For answer, Birbal smiled at her kindly, and told her she could go home happily now.

"How did you do it, Birbal?" asked one of the courtiers, the moment her back was turned. He was present at the time and had heard everything.

"Well," explained Birbal, smiling. "I wrote to that judge and bluffed him. I told him he was due to be given a higher post soon. So he gave back the old woman's jewels."

"No doubt, to avoid trouble, which could have spoilt his chances of getting the job," guessed the courtier at once.

But Birbal frowned. "Trouble! He's still in trouble. He will be punished. Judges must always be honest," he stated firmly and walked away.

The Dishonest Tailor

During their many discussions, Akbar and Birbal would at times think differently on certain matters. They would argue, and quite often each would try to prove himself right.

One day they talked about dishonesty.

"Who, would you say, are the most dishonest people?" asked Akbar.

"I think tailors, goldsmiths and traders are the most dishonest," answered Birbal. "A tailor will always steal a piece of his customer's cloth. A goldsmith will always help himself to some of his customer's gold. A trader will always overcharge on the goods he sells."

"But, I feel, if one is careful, it is possible to stop such things from happening," pointed out Akbar. "For instance, take the case of a tailor! Give a tailor a job to do. But instead of letting him take your cloth home, make him work in your presence. That way, you will make sure he cannot steal a piece."

But Birbal shook his head. "I cannot agree with you, Sire! I think a tailor will still find a way of stealing a piece."

The two decided to test and see who was right. Accordingly, a tailor was sent for. He was given a piece of silk, such as the queen only wore, and was ordered to make a blouse for Her Majesty. The cloth was enough to make two blouses, but this was not pointed out to the tailor.

Instead, Birbal said to him: "You will not be allowed to take this cloth home. You must stay here at the palace and finish the job. Start tomorrow! You will be paid well."

The tailor readily agreed. The next morning he arrived at the palace, and was soon settled in a room, with all the things he needed for his work, while a guard was placed outside the door, to keep a watch on him.

The tailor began to cut, and clip, and stitch. He could hardly stop admiring the rare quality of the silk. 'Truly fit for a queen!' he thought.

However, when evening came he had not finished. As such, he was told that he would have to spend the night at the palace. He must continue working, till the blouse was ready. Since he did not return home that night, early next morning his wife sent their small son to find out what had happened.

The guard at the door allowed the boy to enter the room where his father was.

"Abba!" spoke the boy. "Amma has sent me to find out if you are all right."

"Of course, I am all right," snapped the tailor. "Tell your Amma I will return home this evening, as soon as I finish this work."

"You are taking very long, Abba!" remarked the boy cheekily. "As Amma says, no wonder we are so poor! It is because you stitch so slowly."

"Don't you dare be so bold," scolded the tailor in anger. "Remember, whom you are talking to!" And taking up one of his shoes, he flung it at his son.

The boy laughed, stepping aside quickly. As the shoe missed him and landed on the floor, he picked it up and raced out of the room.

"Now you will not get back your shoe, Abba!" he called over his shoulder.

"Catch him! Catch that boy!" shouted the tailor to the guard.

But his son had already gone, while the guard quite rocked with laughter at the joke.

The tailor resumed his work. Early that evening the blouse was ready. Birbal had it sent to the queen, who after trying it on, sent a message to say that it fitted her well. Akbar sent for the tailor and paid him his dues. As the tailor was about to

leave, Akbar asked him if he had used the entire piece of silk to make the blouse.

"But, of course, Sire!" answered the tailor, sounding quite hurt. "We tailors are all honest. If there was any cloth left, I would surely have returned it."

"Well, that proves me right," said Akbar to Birbal, when the tailor hade gone.

But Birbal answered, with a shake of the head: "Let us wait and see who is right, Sire!"

Two days later, one of the queen's maids went shopping. On her return, excitedly she informed her mistress:

"My lady, would you believe it? But I just saw a woman in the market. She was wearing a blouse, exactly like the one that tailor made for you a few days ago."

"Really! Now how can that be? The cloth for my garments is supposed to be woven only for me," said the queen, and, very upset, off she went to Akbar to report the matter.

When Akbar told Birbal what the queen had to say, Birbal guessed who the woman in the market had been. At once he sent for the tailor.

"Look here!" he addressed him strictly. "One of

the queen's maids has seen a woman in the market, wearing a blouse like the one you made for Her Majesty. Since Her Majesty's clothes are made from special materials, how can you explain this?"

The tailor pretended to be surprised. But Birbal challenged him.

"No doubt about it, that woman was your wife!" he announced. "If you do not speak the truth, I will have you punished."

Now, the tailor grew afraid and began to weep.

"Please do not punish me, Sir!" he begged. "I did steal a piece of that cloth. I hid it in one of my shoes, which I flung at my son, when he came to see me. I had planned it all with my wife and my son, in advance."

Birbal was not surprised. "I well know how you did it," he answered calmly, "When the guard told me about that incident, I guessed you had hidden the cloth in your shoe." And with that he dismissed the tailor in disgust.

"So you were right, after all," admitted Akbar to Birbal later. "I wonder; if I will ever be able to prove you wrong!" he added, and laughed.

The Most Foolish Men in Delhi

Though Akbar had spoken in fun, the idea of trying to prove Birbal wrong in some matters greatly pleased him. But since Birbal never seemed to do anything wrong, Akbar decided to set him a task, which he felt would be impossible to carry out. That way, he would have the satisfaction of winning. It would be a great joke, Akbar thought.

As such, he said to Birbal one day: "Birbal, I have met the wisest men in the kingdom. Now I would like to meet the most foolish. Do you think you can find me the six most foolish men in Delhi?"

"I'll try, Sire'." answered Birbal, not one bit troubled by this strange request.

Birbal set out early one morning, therefore. He walked through the streets of Delhi, looking around carefully. Very soon he spotted a man. The fellow was lying on his back in a puddle of water, his arms stretched wide above his head, some three feet apart. Every now and then he waved his legs in the air.

"What are you trying to do?" asked Birbal, going up to him.

"I am trying to stand up. I slipped and fell into this puddle, while I was on my way to buy some cloth for my wife," answered the man, waving his legs about some more.

"Why don't you use your hands, then?" suggested Birbal. "You would find it easier to get up'."

"But I cannot do that!" cried the man. "If I change the position of my hands, I will lose the measurement of the length of cloth my wife wants."

"In that case, my friend!" pointed out Birbal with a smile. "You will not be able to stand up, I am sure. But I will help you." And at once he grabbed the fellow by the hair, and set him on his feet.

"Thank you! Thank you!'" said the man gratefully, his arms still above his head. "My name is Karim. You have certainly been of great help to me."

"Well, you can help me, too, Karim," said Birbal. "Would you come with me, please?"

"But, certainly!" agreed Karim, and because he was so very foolish, he did not even trouble to ask why.

As they went along, Birbal next saw a man riding a horse. The man had a bundle of straw on his head.

"Why do you carry that straw on your head?" Birbal went up to him to ask. "Can't you keep it on the horse's back, behind you?"

"But I cannot do that, Sir!" answered the man. "This horse is so old and so weak, it might die with the extra weight. Already, it has to carry me."

Birbal almost laughed at the great foolishness of the man. 'Do you think, that by carrying the straw on your head, it takes the weight off the horse's back?" he almost asked him. But, instead, he said :

"My good man, what is your name ?"

"My name is Hasan," came the answer.

"In that case, Hasan, you are just the person I am looking for. Please follow me !"

Without a murmur, Hasan turned his horse round. He began to ride behind Birbal and Karim, the bundle of straw still on his head.

Now, as they continued on their way, Birbal, all of a sudden spotted a man, racing along in their direction. He was talking aloud to himself. He came at such speed, that before Birbal could step aside, the man crashed into him, almost knocking him off his feet.

"What are you doing ? Can't you see where you are going ?" demanded Birbal angrily.

"And can't you see where you are going ?" flung back the man, equally angry. "I was chasing the sound of my own voice. I would have caught up with it, but for you coming in my way !"

"Well, don't be worried !" said Birbal, smiling now. "Come with me. I will help you to catch the sound of your voice."

"You promise ?" asked the man, in some relief.

"I certainly do !" replied Birbal, and as the man joined him, they all moved on.

Since he had found three, Birbal now began to search for the fourth most foolish man in Delhi. But though he searched all that day, he was not able to find such a man. As night began to fall, he made his way back to the palace, with the three most foolish men still following him—Karim with his arms still above his head, Hasan still riding his horse, with the bundle of straw still on his head, while the third man was still trying to catch up with the sound of his own voice.

However, as Birbal wondered what he should do, suddenly, very near the palace gates, he noticed a man. The man was quite bent in half, looking for something under a street light.

"What are you searching for?" Birbal asked the man.

"I have lost my diamond ring. Somewhere out there in the darkness!" answered the man, pointing to a dark spot far away from where he stood. "But since I could not see over there, I am looking for my ring here, as there is light."

"Ah!" cried Birbal. "If you would but come with me, I will help you to find your ring."

The man agreed most readily, and quite pleased with himself now, Birbal entered the palace gates, followed by the four.

"Sire!" he announced, as he lined them up before Akbar, which included Hasan's horse, as well, for Hasan was still seated on it. "I have brought you the four most foolish men in the city of Delhi."

"Really! And how did you judge they were the most foolish?" Akbar wanted to know, amused to see the curious lot that stood before him.

"Why! By their actions, of course!" answered Birbal, and he went on to point out and give an account of each.

"Very good!" said Akbar, when he had finished. "But I asked you to bring me the six most foolish men, not four!" and his eyes twinkled at the thought, that at last he had managed to trap Birbal. No doubt, Birbal had not been able to find the last two.

However, Birbal remained quite calm, as he announced: "If you look carefully, Sire, you will see six, as you asked for! The last two most foolish men in Delhi are you and I. You because you set me such a foolish task. I because I foolishly carried it out. that makes six, doesn't it?"

"It does! It certainly does!" agreed Akbar, enjoying the joke hugely. And he laughed, till the tears quite rolled down his cheeks.

Unlucky Chand

While Birbal helped Akbar in all matters, at times he also helped him to change his mind. This was on those occasions when Akbar wished to act unwisely, or do something foolish.

One such happening concerned a merchant named Chand. It was said by all that Chand was unlucky. Whoever saw his face on a morning, would have bad luck for the rest of that day.

Akbar got to hear of Chand. He thought the stories about him were unkind and unjust. So he sent for Chand, to judge for himself.

Chand arrived early one morning. Akbar received him kindly, and began to talk to him. But as he questioned Chand about himself, one of the queen's maids arrived all of a sudden.

"Sire, I am sorry to disturb you!" she said, sounding quite worried. "But Her Majesty has suddenly taken ill. Please do come at once."

Excusing himself, Akbar hurried away. When he reached the queen's bedside, he found that his wife was indeed quite ill. Akbar was upset. He sent for the court physician, who soon arrived and examined the queen.

"Sire, it is only a small illness," he declared. "I am ordering some medicines for Her Majesty. She will be well very soon. Do not worry!"

Though that certainly set Akbar's mind at rest, he remained by the queen's bedside, till he was quite certain she was out of danger. By the time he thought fit to leave, it was near lunchtime.

Meanwhile Chand had waited. Akbar had quite forgotten about Chand. But as he came out of the queen's private chamber, he remembered, and hurried along to join him. On the way he was stopped by one of his attendants.

"Sire!" said the man. "Your lunch awaits you. If you delay, I fear the food will be spoiled."

"All right! I'm coming," answered Akbar. He would talk to Chand when he had finished eating, he now decided.

However, when he reached the royal dining hall and sat down to his meal, Akbar found the food was already cold and tasteless.

"What is the meaning of this?" he demanded of the servants who were waiting on him. "How dare you serve me food of this kind! Take it away at once! Prepare something tasty, or I will have all of you punished." And in a huff he stamped out of the dining hall.

Akbar now made up his mind to finish his chat with Chand, while a fresh meal was being got ready for him. But he was very hungry. He grew more cross, as a result, and began to find fault.

'Certainly, this Chand is to blame!' he said to himself. 'I had hardly begun speaking to him, when the queen fell ill. Now my lunch is ruined. What people say is quite right. Chand is unlucky. He is a danger to all. He must be put in prison, in a cell all by himself. That way, no one will see his face, and suffer bad luck.'

With that, most angry, Akbar sent for his jailer. He ordered that Chand be locked up right away. Poor Chand was most surprised and upset, when the jailer appeared before him suddenly, and marched him off. To Chand's good luck, on the way, they passed Birbal.

"Great, kind Birbal!" called out Chand at once. "Please save me. His Majesty has ordered me to be put in prison. He says, as do so many others, that my face has brought him bad luck."

Birbal was sorry to hear this. Taking Chand aside, he whispered in his ear. After which, he ordered the jailer to take Chand to meet the king.

"But don't tell His Majesty that these are my instructions," he added.

Meanwhile Akbar had finished eating the fresh meal that had been prepared for him. Quite satisfied now, he felt much better. In fact, he was in quite a good mood. Though he looked up angrily, as the jailer led Chand in to meet him.

"What is the meaning of this?" he demanded. "How dare you bring this man to me! I ordered him to be put in prison."

"Sire!" answered the jailer. "This man desired to meet you, before I put him in prison. He pleaded so much, I could hardly refuse."

Of course, by now, poor Chand was on his knees before the king. With folded hands, he begged Akbar for mercy.

"Sire!" he said, when Akbar told him he could speak. "You are punishing me, because you say my face brought you bad luck today. But consider my position! Your face has brought me bad luck, too. After meeting you, I am now to be put in prison."

Akbar at once realised he had acted unwisely. He began to laugh now.

"My good man," he said to Chand. "What you have just said is very clever. I agree to spare you. But I think I can guess who taught you to say that."

As he was set free, Chand thanked Akbar warmly and left. Soon after, when Akbar met Birbal, he remarked, with a knowing look :

"Birbal, you are smart, I must say ! But I am glad you correct me, when I act unwisely, at times."

Birbal's answer was simply to smile.

The Prince and the Traveller

One day Prince Suryasingh of Manipur was on his way to Delhi for some important business. Since this business was a secret, the prince was travelling alone, without his followers or attendants. He was a brave young man, and was not afraid to be on his own.

However, as he rode along, suddenly he came across a fellow traveller. The man was seated by the side of the road. He looked very sad. Thinking he was in trouble, the prince got off his horse and went up to the man.

"My friend," he said to him kindly, "you look very sad. Are you in trouble?"

"Sir," answered the traveller, beginning to weep, "I am indeed in trouble. I was on my way to Delhi for some urgent work, when some robbers attacked me. They stole my horse and my money. I have nothing left. I have not eaten since yesterday. I do not have the strength to even walk."

"Well, do not worry," said the prince generously. "I will give you to eat. And since I am on my way to Delhi, too, I will give you a lift."

The traveller was very grateful. Quickly he ate the food which Prince Suryasingh gave him. Then saying he was feeling much better, he got up behind the prince on his horse, and together they rode along.

Soon they reached Delhi. As they entered the city, Prince Suryasingh got off his horse, and made to help the traveller down, too.

To his surprise, the traveller refused to move.

"Why should I get down?" he said to the prince coldly. "This is my horse. I have given you a lift. Now you go your way, and let me ride on."

"But you know this is not your horse," cried the prince, quite amazed. He realised now the traveller had been out to cheat him. The story he had told, was part of a plan to steal his horse. For certain, the man was a thief.

Prince Suryasingh decided to be firm. "Look here!" he said sternly. "You well know this horse is mine. You had better get off. I shall not let you get away with this."

"If this horse is yours, you will have to prove it," answered the traveller cunningly.

But, as he tried to ride on, Prince Suryasingh quickly grabbed the reins, and sprang up on the horse behind him. Taken by surprise, the traveller could do nothing, except take the prince along with him. The prince was also helpless. He had to go the way the traveller took him.

However, the prince was waiting for the right moment. And no sooner did they reach a crowded spot, than he began to shout.

"Help! Help!" he cried. "This man is stealing my horse."

But at this point the traveller began to shout, too. He cried out that the horse was his, and the prince was trying to steal it. Hearing them a crowd soon gathered round. The people demanded to know what was the matter. But on being told different stories by both parties, none could decide whom the horse belonged to. So it was settled that the matter be taken before Birbal.

Thus, soon Prince Suryasingh and the traveller had to repeat their stories to Birbal. Birbal listened carefully. When they had finished speaking, he said to them:

"Leave the horse here, and return tomorrow! I will let you know what I decide."

As the two went away, and the crowd left, too, Birbal called one of his servants.

"Take the horse and go after those two," he ordered the man. "Make sure they don't see, but allow the horse to follow them for a bit. When you are certain which one of the two it is following, take the horse to the palace stables and leave it there."

The servant did as he was told. He soon noticed that the horse followed the prince. When he was fully satisfied about this, he took the horse to the palace stables, and kept it along with the other royal horses. After that he went and reported to Birbal what he had found out.

Now Birbal had some proof that the horse belonged to the prince. However, when the two arrived the next day, as a further test, he ordered them to be taken separately to the stables, to point out the horse. While the prince was able to know his horse at once, the traveller chose the wrong horse.

Birbal was now quite certain that the horse belonged to the prince. At once he ordered that it be returned to him. To the traveller, he said sternly:

"Confess the truth at once! Or you will be put in prison!"

Quite trembling, the man now admitted he had tried to steal the prince's horse. Birbal gave him a good scolding, and let him go.

"Prince Suryasingh," he addressed the prince next. "You must be more careful in future. Think well, before you offer to help a stranger."

But the prince cried out in amazement: "You called me by my name! I never told you who I was. How do you know me?"

"I make it my business to know all important people," answered Birbal quietly. "I know you the moment I saw you. I guessed you were speaking the truth. A prince of your wealth would not try to steal a horse. But, as you know, everything must be proved. You proved you were the owner of the horse, by pointing it out in a group of other horses. Yesterday, unknown to you and that man, the horse proved it was owned by you." And he went on to tell how this had been done.

"You really are a wonderful man!" cried Prince Suryasingh, when Birbal had finished. "I am glad I have met you... In fact, I feel rather grateful to that cunning fellow. If it hadn't been for him, I would not have had the chance," he ended, with a laugh.

Birbal makes Enemies

Birbal grew more and more famous. In time, he became the king's favourite. Akbar would consult him in all matters, and gave him great powers. Some of the courtiers and ministers, as a result, grew jealous. These thought that Birbal would become greater than them some day. They feared they would lose their places at court, and perhaps be sent away.

As such, these soon began to discuss amongst themselves.

"The king depends on Birbal in all matters," remarked one. "He always consults him, instead of us."

"Yes, and that Birbal certainly has an answer for everything," said another.

"Well we would have answers, too, if we were asked, and were given time to think," put in a third. "But perhaps our king feels that Birbal is the only clever person here! Perhaps, he thinks we are all fools."

"Well, I feel, we should all go and ask the king frankly, why he does not consult us these days," suggested a fourth.

"Yes that is a very good idea," agreed everyone, and they went at once in a body to meet the king.

"Sire!" they said to him. "We notice you have stopped seeking our help these days. You do not ask our opinions any more. You only consult Birbal. Do you think Birbal is the only person who can help you?"

Akbar guessed at once that these courtiers and ministers were jealous. But since he did not wish to upset them more, he did not accuse them. He smiled and tried to explain.

"Well, the reason is quite simple. You are often not able to help me. Birbal always can. So I have got into the habit of consulting him at all times."

But he could see they were not satisfied. Akbar, therefore, decided to prove it to them. Sending for Birbal, he asked the group when Birbal arrived:

"Can any of you tell me, how many sparrows are there to be found in this city?"

The courtiers and ministers present were surprised to be asked such a question. They looked at each other, quite puzzled.

"We really don't know!" they said at last. "Do give us time, sire! We will find out."

But Akbar now turned to Birbal. "Can you tell me, Birbal, how many sparrows are there to be found in this city?"

"Yes, sire!" answered Birbal at once, to the amazement of the others. "There are seventy thousand five hundred and fifty-four sparrows to be found in this city."

"Really!" cried one of the courtiers, with a cunning smile. "Anyone can give an answer like that. How do we know you are correct? There may be more; there may be less."

"You are quite right. There may be more or less,"

nodded Birbal, not one bit worried. "The reason for that is quite simple. Many sparrows have left the city to visit other places. So I have not counted those. Many from other places have come to visit this city. I have not counted those, either."

The courtiers and ministers guessed at once that such a smart answer made it impossible for them to check if Birbal was right. They grew silent and angry. But Akbar began to laugh.

"You see!" he cried. "Birbal always has an answer ready. I think you know now why I consult him always."

But though they said nothing, these courtiers and ministers were not satisfied. They continued to grumble amongst themselves, while they began to dislike Birbal.

Akbar sets a Task

Akbar soon got to know that some of his courtiers and ministers had become Birbal's enemies. Since he well know the reason for this, he decided to set a task, which would prove to these people that Birbal was better than they were.

Akbar had got to hear that a caravan of merchants had arrived, and had camped outside the gates of the city. As such, he sent for those courtiers and ministers who were Birbal's enemies.

"I understand that a caravan of merchants has camped outside the gates of the city," he said to them. "I want you to go and inspect this caravan. Report to me about it."

The courtiers and ministers left to do as they had been asked. Meanwhile Akbar sent for Birbal and set him the same task.

Later, the courtiers and ministers returned, to report what they had discovered.

"Well," asked Akbar, "how many merchants were there in this caravan?"

"About twenty, Sire!" answered one of the group promptly.

"What good were these merchants trading in?" asked Akbar next.

"They were trading in several items," answered another.

"What sort of items? Let me know exactly!" Akbar spoke with some impatience.

"Well, Sire!" replied a third. "There were several cloth merchants and several dealers in grain. There were a few oil merchants, and one selling animal skins."

"Did they have any horses?" Akbar wanted to know next.

"Yes, there were several horses," the group answered together.

"Any camels?"

The group of courtiers and ministers looked doubtful. "We did not see any," they said with some hesitation.

"Do you have anything else to say?" asked Akbar sharply, not at all satisfied with their answers.

All now shook their heads, upon which Akbar sent for Birbal.

"Birbal!" he addressed him, as Birbal came into the room. "I asked you to report to me about that caravan of merchants camped outside the gates of the city. Have you been able to find out about them?"

"Yes, Sire!" answered Birbal. "I have just returned after meeting the marchants."

"How many merchants were there?" asked Akbar.

"There were twenty-two," replied Birbal.

"What was their business?"

"Eleven were cloth merchants, Sire! Seven were dealers in grain, which included one flour merchant.

Three were oil merchants, and one was selling animal skins." Birbal ticked the numbers off on his fingers as he spoke.

"Did they have any horses?" continued Akbar.

"Yes, Sire! They had twenty-five horses with them. Ten were black. Eight were white. Three were brown and white. The balance four were black and white.

"Were there any other animals?"

"Yes, Sire! There were five camels. One had an injured foreleg."

"Have you anything else to report?"

"Yes, Sire! The merchants sent you their greetings. They will be here for a week, after which they plan to move on."

"Very good!" said Akbar, with a smile now. He was very pleased that Birbal had proved himself superior to the others.

"And now!" he turned to the group to say. "I think you will understand why I depend so much on Birbal."

The group of enemies were, of course, most angry by now though they well knew they had no reason to be. It was their own fault, if they did not take note of things, as carefully as Birbal did. However, in their jealousy, these now planned to trap Birbal. They took every chance they got, to ask him all sorts of difficult and tricky questions. They hoped Birbal would say something in reply, that would make the king lose trust in him

But Birbal always managed to answer their questions very cleverly, while Akbar's trust in him remained as firm as ever.